Reprinted by HENRY FORD from
McGUFFEY'S FIRST ECLECTIC READER
1930

ECLECTIC EDUCATIONAL SERIES.

McGUFFEY'S

NEW

FIRST ECLECTIC READER:

FOR YOUNG LEARNERS.

By WM. H. McGUFFEY, LL. D.

NEW-YORK ∴ CINCINNATI ∴ CHICAGO

AMERICAN BOOK COMPANY

FROM THE PRESS OF
VAN ANTWERP, BRAGG, & CO.

PUBLISHERS' NOTICE.

The widely extended approval bestowed upon the ECLEC-
TIC EDUCATIONAL SERIES for many years has given them a
constantly increasing demand. Their sale is not equalled by
that of any similar text-books. The Series includes:

> McGuffey's Revised Speller, Readers, and Charts,
> Ray's New Arithmetics,
> Ray's New Algebras,
> Eclectic School Geometry,
> White's New Arithmetics,
> Milne's Inductive Arithmetics,
> Milne's Inductive Algebra,
> Schuyler's Complete Algebra,
> Schuyler's Elementary Geometry,
> Harvey's Revised Grammars,
> Holbrook's Normal Grammars,
> New Eclectic Geographies,
> New Eclectic Penmanship,
> Eclectic United States History,
> Eclectic Primary History,
> Ridpath's United States Histories,
> Thalheimer's Histories,
> Kidd's New Elocution,
> Murdoch's Analytic Elocution,
> Eclectic System of Drawing,
> Forbriger's Drawing Tablets,
> Eclectic Complete Book-keeping,
> Eclectic Physiology and Hygiene,
> Etc., Etc.

All persons ordering, in order to avoid possible mistakes
in titles of books, should consult our latest *Catalogue and Price
List of the Eclectic Educational Series*, which will be forwarded,
postpaid, by mail, on application.

AMERICAN BOOK COMPANY,

NEW-YORK ·:· CINCINNATI ·:· CHICAGO.

THE ALPHABET.

a	A	*a*	n	N	*n*
b	B	*b*	o	O	*o*
c	C	*c*	p	P	*p*
d	D	*d*	q	Q	*q*
e	E	*e*	r	R	*r*
f	F	*f*	s	S	*s*
g	G	*g*	t	T	*t*
h	H	*h*	u	U	*u*
i	I	*i*	v	V	*v*
j	J	*j*	w	W	*w*
k	K	*k*	x	X	*x*
l	L	*l*	y	Y	*y*
m	M	*m*	z	Z	*z*

A a	AX ax
B b	BOX box
C c	CAT cat
D d	DOG dog
E e	ELK elk
F f	FAN fan
G g	GIRL girl
H h	HEN hen
I i	INK ink
J j	JUG jug

K k	KID kid	P p	PIG pig
L l	LARK lark	Q q	QUAIL quail
M m	MAN man	R r	RAT rat
N n	NUT nut	S s	SUN sun
O o	OX ox	T t	TUB tub

U	URN	X	EX
u	urn	x	ex
V	VINE	Y	YOKE
v	vine	y	yoke
W	WREN	Z	ZEBRA
w	wren	z	zebra

MODEL PRONOUNCING EXERCISE,

Embracing all the words found in Lesson I, on the following page.

I	in	do	we	he
it	on	go	am	my
is	an	no	ox	up

LESSON I.

Let the child spell each word in the line, then read the line.

SPELL.	READ.
is it an ox	Is it an ox?
it is an ox	It is an ox.
it is my ox	It is my ox.
do we go	Do we go?
do we go up	Do we go up?
we do go up	We do go up.
am I in	Am I in?
am I in it	Am I in it?
I am in it	I am in it.

LESSON II.*

Is it an ax?
It is an ax.
It is my ax.
Is it by me?
My ax is by me. So it is.

Is he in?
He is in.
Is he by me?
Do we go in?

It is I.
It is he.
We do it.
Do as we do.

* Spell each word in the line, then read the line, as in Lesson I.

LESSON III.*

A sly hen.

Can she fly?

A bad dog.

It bit a man

A big ox.

Let him go.

A fat pig.

Can it run?

A red cow.

Has she hay?

* Spell each word in the line; then read, as in Lesson I.

LESSON IV.*

Can the cat
get the rat?

See the rat.
Was it hid?

See the kid.
Can it run?

A sly fox.
He had a hen.

An old ape.
Can he hop?

* Spell each word in the line; then read, as in Lesson I

LESSON V.

Is it a bed?	A fan for Ann.
It is a bed.	Can you fan me?
Is it for me?	I can fan you.
It is for me.	You can fan me.
Kit is on my bed.	You do fan me.

LESSON VI

I see a nag.	I see a pig.
Do you see it?	How fat it is!
Yes, yes, I do.	Can the pig run?
The nag can run.	It can not run.
See it, O, see it run!	It is too fat to run.

LESSON VII.

An old log hut.
A new log hut.
Is it for me?
Is it for you?
It is for us.

See my fat ox.
Is it an old ox?
It is an old ox.
It is not a red ox.
It is a dun ox.

A sly old ape.
It has a nut.
Get it for me.
May I get it?
Yes, if you can.

O, see the fly!
How it can fly!
It bit an old ox
Can the fly run?
Yes! run, fly, run!

LESSON VIII.

Is it a cow?
It is a cow.
It is my cow.
She has no hay.
Let her be fed.

I see a tub.
The tub is big.
Can you use it?
O yes, I can.
I can use it.

O, see my cat!
He is on a mat.
He saw a rat.
The rat saw him.
The rat ran off.

See my new top.
How it can hum.
You may get one.
Do not beg one.
I do not beg.

LESSON IX.

See! a new cap.
A cap for you.
I had a cap.
It was new.
Now it is old.

See the big kid.
It is my pet kid.
Is it not shy?
My kid is shy.
Let us go out.

It is an elk.
The elk is sly.
The dog saw him.
He saw the dog.
The elk ran off.

See the dog run.
It saw a man.
The man did say,
    pup, pup, pup!
The dog ran off.

LESSON X.

I can see you, cat.
Do you see me?
The cat is on my
 new fur cap.
Get off, old cat.

I see a dog.
I can see a pup.
Do you see me?
The dog and pup
 may run all day.

Ned and his nag.
Can the nag run?
Can it run far?
O yes, the nag can
 run; so can Ned.

See the old hen.
Is she not fat?
Can the hen fly?
Can she fly far?
The hen can fly.

LESSON XI.

I see an old cat.
The old cat is by
her pet kit.
The cat and kit
are on a rug.

A sly old fox, and
a fat old hen.
The fox did try to
get the hen.
Did the hen fly?

dog	boy	get
log	joy	let
hog	toy	set
fog	coy	bet

Do you see the boy and his dog?
Is it a dog, or is it a fox?
Is it a fox? O no, it is a dog.
The dog can run; so can the boy.
Now, Tom, let us see you run.

LESSON XII.

bee   the   do

see   can   him

hum   fly   boy

bud   you   joy

Do you see the bee?   Is it on the bud?
O yes! I see the bee.   It is on the bud.
Can the bee fly?   Can it hum too?
The bee can fly and hum.   Ah! so it can.

---

me   can   see

so   hop   yes

ah   Ned   far

oh   Tom   you

Ned, can you hop?   Can you hop far?
Yes, I can hop.   I can hop so far.
Can you hop, Tom?   Can you hop to me?
Yes; see me.   I can hop to you, Ned.
I can hop as far as you can.
Ah! so you can.   Now let us hop.

LESSON XIII.

Ann	ten	old
are	six	you
am	big	how
as	but	why

Ann, how old are you? I am six.
Are you but six? Why, I am ten.
But you are not as big as I am.

Ned	too	but
Hal	was	bad
pet	box	odd
pig	boy	who

Ned has a pet pig. Do you see it?
Is it not an odd pet? Can it run?
Hal has a pet hen. His hen can run.
Can she fly? Can she fly or run far?
Ned, who has the pig, is a bad boy.
Hal is a big boy, but not a bad boy.

Simple and familiar words, not found in the reading lesson,
are occasionally introduced into the spelling list.

LESSON XIV.

lap   its   as

red   the   one

did   put   was

bid   and   Ann

Ann bid her dog put up its red paw.
The dog did as it was bid. It put its
   paw in her lap. Did you not see it?
It put up no paw but the red one.

rat   far   fee

get   sly   lee

has   run   see

dog   you   bee

Can the dog get the rat? See, see,
   how sly he is.
Ah, now he has the rat. Did you see
   the rat run? Did it run far?
The dog did not let it run far. The
   dog did get the rat.

LESSON XV.

is	fat	let	lay
us	sty	fed	ray
my	not	bit	say
the	pig	now	pay

I see a dog. The dog bit my pig.
Is my pig in the sty? Let us see.
The dog can not see my pig now.
Let the fat old pig be fed.

boy	lid	off	ill
put	sat	out	pill
box	cat	ran	kill
hen	the	eye	mill

A boy put a cat and a hen in a box.
The boy sat on the lid of the box.
The cat bit the hen; and the hen put
  out the eye of the cat.
The boy got off the lid of the box. The
  cat got out and ran off.

LESSON XVI.

ill	as	she	lie
too	the	put	die
get	run	hay	pie
hen	sun	was	hie

The hen was too ill to get up; but she was not so ill as to die.

The hen was put on the hay. She was put on the hay, in the sun.

lap	tip	lie	all
pet	she	ear	tall
dog	kid	eat	call
Ann	her	one	ball

Ann had a pet lap-dog. She let it lie on her bed.

She fed it of all she had to eat.

Her dog was not as big as a kid; not as big as a kid one day old.

The tip of one ear was red.

LESSON XVII.

let   us   our   fay

hot   fun   out   hay

dog   can   new   nay

hog   put   with   day

It is a hot day.   Let us go out.
Let us go out with our dog.
We can go to the new-cut hay.
We can put hay on our dog for fun.

all   oh   fit   the

for   aid   we   this

his   bid   are   that

God   our   eye   then

O! my God, let me do no sin.   Aid
  me to do as I am bid.
Our God can see all we do.   Let all
  I do be fit for his eye.
Let me do to all as I am bid.   Let
  me do as all are bid to do to me.

LESSON XVIII.

fox	fat	ran	fly
old	rat	hen	sly
say	cat	dog	try
may	hat	saw	cry

The fox may say: I am sly.
I had an old fat hen.   A man saw me.
A dog saw me.   I ran and hid.
I am so sly, a man can not get me.
A dog can not get me, if I run.

sip	few	to	lie
lap	hew	do	fie
not	pew	rug	die
and	mew	sun	hie

The cat may say: I do not sip, I lap.
I can run.   See, I can get a rat.
I can get a fly, if it is not too far off.
I can mew, and I can lie in the sun.
I can lie on a rug, or on the hay.

LESSON XIX.

far	lay	ten	use
jar	say	hen	man
car	may	pen	egg
bar	play	wen	eggs

The hen may say: I can run. I can
fly, but not far up in the air.
I can lay eggs, and am of use to man.
The fox and the rat may get me; but
if I see the fox or rat, I run off.

see	joy	tea	rose
bee	toy	kill	dose
flee	coy	dew	hose
glee	boy	new	nose

The bee may say: I fly in the air. I
sip, but I do not get in the tea-cup.
I sip the dew on the rose, and fly off.
Boy, do not try to kill me; for I am
of use to man.

LESSON XX.

Ann	fed	see	you
Tom	fox	big	with
Tray	rat	cow	will
tell	dog	him	call

It is old Tray. Tray is a big dog.
Do you see our old Tray, the big dog?
He is fed by Tom and Ann.
He will run if Ann and Tom call him.
Now, Tray, let me see how you can run.

Sly	pig	but	eel
man	hen	let	peel
met	how	and	heel
mud	now	why	feel

Sly will do as he is bid. He is a pet dog.
He will run at a pig or a cow.
He will run at a fox or an ox.
He will run at a hen or a rat.
A fox or a pig will not run at Sly.

LESSON XXI.

get	try	but	eel
did	use	you	feel
can	saw	low	heel
mud	now	may	peel

I saw an eel in the mud, and I did try
　to get it, but did not.

May I try now?　No, it is of no use.

It is low in the mud.　You can see it;
　but you can not get it if you try.

let	kit	do	are
she	am	the	now
but	her	not	why
has	bid	will	may

Let the cat be: she has a kit.

Do not go to her now, but sit by me.

Why may I not go to her now?

Do not ask why, but do as you are bid.

I will do as I am bid.　I will not go.

LESSON XXII.

eat	free	who	lest	egg
seat	tree	why	best	eggs
heat	trees	what	nest	bird
neat	spree	when	nests	birds

What is in the tree?
A nest. A nest is in the tree.

What are in the nest?
Eggs. Eggs are in the nest.
The nest is in the tree.

What are in the eggs?
Birds. Birds are in the eggs.
The eggs are in the nest.
The nest is in the tree.

SPELLING is of the utmost importance in securing the progress of the young learner in *reading*.

LESSON XXIII.

air	rice	rat
fair	vice	rats
hair	nice	cats
pair	mice	hats

A dog will bark and run and play.
A cow will give milk if well fed.
A hen will lay eggs on the hay.
A sly cat will get mice and rats.
A bird will sing in the tree all day.

cart	tree	egg
bark	bird	eggs
hark	sing	give
mark	milk	horse

A horse can draw the cart and man.
A bee will fly in the air and hum.
An ox or a cow will eat hay.
A fox will eat hens. He will eat mice
and rats too. Ah, the sly old fox!

Always see that the spelling lessons are thoroughly studied.

LESSON XXIV.

Ma-ry	cov-er	po-ny	lit-tle
Lu-cy	hov-er	bo-ny	ket-tle
Kit-ty	lov-er	co-ny	set-tle
la-dy	cov-et	ho-ly	met-tle

big	tail	li-on
cow	kill	Zi-on
paw	long	let-ter
blow	mane	bet-ter

Is it a dog, or a cow, or an ox?
No; it is not a dog, or a cow, or an ox.
It is a li-on. See his long mane and tail.
The li-on can kill a man. He can kill a
man with one blow of his big paw.

Many words of two syllables are more simple than some mono-
syllables of three, four, and five letters.

LESSON XXV.

get	six	what	lie
got	you	when	die
bed	mix	where	pie
sun	now	play	fie

Get up, Lu-cy. Do not lie in bed now.
It is day, and the sun is up. Ma-ry got
 up at six, and is out at play.
Up, up, Lu-cy, why do you lie in bed?
Get up, Lu-cy, and go out to Ma-ry.

red	new	the	came
has	Ann	this	same
box	was	that	fame
you	said	then	tame

Ma-ry has a new box, a big box.
Let us go and see it. The box is red.
Ma-ry said it was for her: so, Ann, it
 can not be for you.
It has M on the cov-er; M for MA-RY.

LESSON XXVI.

air	kite	line
here	gave	new
held	with	rose
hold	when	lit-tle

Here is Tom with his new kite.
Tom said to lit-tle Ned, See my kite!
When it is in the air, you may hold it.
Ned went with Tom, and held the kite.
Tom ran, and the kite rose. Then Tom
gave the line to Ned.

has	one	out
see	two	cap
boy	saw	on-ly
Ned	new	lit-tle

Do you see the boy? It is lit-tle Ned.
Has Ned a new cap? Can you see it?
He is at the pen to see his lit-tle pig.
I saw it fed at one. It is now on-ly two.
Can not the pig get out of its pen?

LESSON XXVII.

sun   see   west

may   how   down

gone   why   kill'ed

came   soon   set-ting

May I get my cap, Ned? We can go and
see the sun set.

See, Ned, how red it is. Why is the set-
ting sun so red?

Will it soon be down in the west?

Yes; the sun will soon set in the west.

A dog saw a rat.

A cat saw it too.

The dog ran for it, but
the cat got it.

How did the cat get the rat?

I will tell you. The sly old cat was hid.

The rat had gone in-to a box; but it
came out of it too soon.

The cat put her paw on it, and killed it.

LESSON XXVIII.

well	find	rose	old
bell	kind	dose	told
sell	mind	nose	cold
tell	blind	hose	bold
fell	grind	pose	scold

old	sick	son
like	care	you
poor	once	take
blind	must	lit-tle

This old man is poor, and ill, and blind.
He is led by his dog, a lit-tle red dog.
Once he was a lit-tle boy, like you; but
   now he is old, and sick, and poor.
He has no son to take care of him.
He must be led by his lit-tle dog.

1st Rd 3

LESSON XXIX.

cart	this	seek
part	that	meek
dart	thou	cheek
tart	there	cheeks

Do you see the new cart and the fork?
Is it a new cart, or is it an old one?
It is a new one, but the fork is old.
A new cart and an old fork.
Do you not like to ride on the cart?

lips	eye	doll
hair	eyes	gave
wax	Jane	small
blue	cheeks	Su-san

Lit-tle Jane Day has a new doll.
She went to see Su-san Page, and Su-san
  gave her this doll.
It is a wax doll, and has blue eyes.
It has red lips and cheeks.
Jane has a small box to put it in.

LESSON XXX.

net   swim   boy
fish   swing   bird
pole   found   lend
line   round   rend

A fish, a net, a pole, and a line.
Can a fish swim? Can it swim far?
Yes, a fish can swim all day.
It can swim as far as a boy can run,
    or a lit-tle bird can fly.

of   sip   air   yet
fly   tea   out   yes
bee   my   why   you
dew   bud   in-to yon

Do you see my cup? A bee is in it.
Why did the bee get in the cup? Is the
    cup for a bee? No, it is not for a bee.
The bee got in-to the cup to sip the tea.
Sip and be off, bee. Fly out in-to the air.
Get in-to the bud, and sip its dew.

LESSON XXXI.

air	duck	fast
fair	luck	past
take	pond	swift
make	bond	swim

Do you see the duck? Can it swim?
Can it fly too? Yes, the duck can fly
    and swim. It can fly far.
It can swim in the pond, or fly in the air.
The duck can swim in the pond all day.

oak	owl	aft-er
saw	gun	raft-er
was	tree	sun-set
said	shot	sit-ting

An owl was sit-ting in an oak tree.
The owl can not see by day; but it can
    see aft-er sun-set.
A boy saw the owl, and said to a man,
    An owl is in the top of the oak.
The man got his gun and shot the owl.

LESSON XXXII.

deer	look	to-ken
beer	brook	sto-len
come	down	bro-ken
some	drink	spo-ken

O Tom, come and look at the deer.
At the deer? Why, Ned, is that a deer?
Yes, it is a deer. Can you not see?
Does not the deer look wild and shy?
He has come down to the brook to drink.

Jane	fall	Sam
poor	left	lit-tle
took	floor	broke
room	head	bro-ken

Poor Jane! Her doll is bro-ken.
Lit-tle Sam Page was in the room.
Jane had left her doll, and he took it.
He let it fall on the floor; and now it
   is bro-ken. Its head is bro-ken off.
Do you not see it on the floor?

LESSON XXXIII.

mel-on	fol-ly	play	o-ver
fel-on	sor-ry	clay	ro-ver
lem-on	sol-id	slay	do-ver
wag-on	cop-y	stay	clo-ver

saw	tree	found
lost	took	ver-y
nest	were	sor-ry
eggs	plum	seems

Has the poor bird lost her nest?
See how sad and sor-ry she seems.
Lit-tle Sam Page saw the nest.
He found it in a plum tree, and took it.
He took it for the eggs that were in it.
Was he not a ver-y, ver-y bad boy?

LESSON XXXIV.

cage	lov-er	cock	ral-ly
sage	cov-er	flock	sal-ly
page	oth-er	dock	par-ry
rage	moth-er	lock	hap-py
gage	broth-er	rock	sap-py

Ann	oh	was
shut	now	then
your	how	hap-py
book	with	moth-er

Ann, you may shut your book now, and
we will go out.

Ann shut her book, put on her hat, and
then she ran for her pet dog.

Ann went with her moth-er; and oh, how
hap-py she was!

LESSON XXXV.

mill	lace	light	laid
mills	face	right	paid
pills	pace	sight	maid
hills	trace	night	braid
rills	place	fight	a-fraid

lark	pur	lie
bark	like	still
hark	mat	place
mark	puss	a-fraid

My fat pup will bark like a dog.

A dog will lie on a mat or a rug.

Puss will pur, if I place her in my lap.

She will lie still in my lap and pur.

Is not puss a-fraid of the pup? No; but
she is a-fraid of the old dog.

LESSON XXXVI.

gan-der	heal	crip-ple	latch
pan-der	peal	dim-ple	catch
dan-der	steal	pim-ple	batch
hin-der	dear	sim-ple	patch
cin-der	clear	rip-ple	match

bird	gets	sings
look	steal	wake
dear	mice	wakes
puss	harm	morn-ing

Do you see puss and our pet bird?

If puss gets the bird, she will kill it.

Puss may catch the mice; for they steal and do us harm.

But puss must not have our dear bird.

It sings and wakes us in the morn-ing.

LESSON XXXVII.

peach	fine	ly-ing
beach	nice	fly-ing
reach	large	fry-ing
teach	what	try-ing

O Ma-ry, do come and see the peach!
Is it not a nice large one?
Is the peach for me, or is it for you?
It is not for you or me.　It is for Lu-cy.
Ah! what a fine peach Lu-cy will have.

ah	eye	o-pen
bird	eyes	ly-ing
were	since	mo-ment
down	clos'ed	sleep-ing

Ah! see the sly puss ly-ing down.
How still she is: her eyes are closed;
　but puss is not sleep-ing.
A mo-ment since her eyes were o-pen.
If she can, she will get our bird.
O! do not let puss get our bird.

LESSON XXXVIII.

coat	lamb	car-ry
goat	jamb	tar-ry
creep	looks	a-ble
sheep	young	sta-ble

Is it a sheep or a goat, or is it a kid?
It is not a kid or a goat. It is a sheep.
Is it an old sheep, or is it a young one?
It is an old sheep.   She has lost her
    lamb.   How sad she looks.

trot	well	come
tail	feed	move
take	eyes	horse
dark	your	small

I like this horse. I like his long tail.
I like his small head and dark eyes.
Come, sir, trot a lit-tle. Move. So! you
    car-ry your tail well.
Your head is up. Now take him to the
    sta-ble, and feed him.

LESSON XXXIX.

one	stop	with
two	rest	black
cow	noon	white
plow	soon	horse

Can the man plow with one horse?
He can plow with one, but he has two.
Ah! so he has; a black and a white one.
Can he plow all day?   O yes; but he
   will stop at noon to rest.

boy	milk	bread
cow	what	but-ter
said	gives	din-ner
your	which	dri-ving

An old man met a boy dri-ving a cow.
The old man said, My lad, what is your
   cow good for?
The boy said, Our cow gives milk.
From milk we make but-ter. We eat
   but-ter with bread for our din-ner.

LESSON XL.

new	good	who
nice	book	aunt
such	kind	your
have	come	gave

Do come, Ma-ry, and see my new book.
A new book, Lu-cy, have you a new book?
O yes, and it is such a nice one too.
Ah! so you have. Who gave it to you?
Your aunt? How kind and good she is.

snow	food	loose
swan	neck	goose
swans	short	riv-er
looks	much	larg-er

This is a swan with its lit-tle swans.
They are in a riv-er. Can you see them?
The swan looks like a goose; but it is
    larg-er, and as white as snow.
It has a long neck and short legs. It
    is not good for food.

LESSON XLI.

bird   rests   gloss-y
come   ri-ses   gold-en
wing   sis-ter   set-tles
thing   pret-ty   shi-ning

See! oh see this shi-ning thing!
It rests its gold-en, gloss-y wing:
Its wing so bright with gold-en light;
Say, is it not a pret-ty sight?

Sis-ter, sis-ter, come and see!
'Tis not a bird, 'tis not a bee:
Ah! it ri-ses, up it goes;
Now it set-tles on a rose.

seal	hear	that	aw-ful
heal	haste	then	law-ful
steal	waste	these	arm-ful
takes	rings	those	let-ting
rakes	sings	there	set-ting
bakes	wings	thine	bet-ting

LESSON XLII.

meet	mu-sic
woods	be-gun
la-bor	morn-ing
du-ty	mo-ments

The lark is up to meet the sun,
    The bee is on the wing;
The ant its la-bor has be-gun,
    The woods with mu-sic ring.

Shall birds, and bees, and ants, be wise,
    While I my mo-ments waste?
O let me with the morn-ing rise,
    And to my du-ty haste.

fees	goods	why	sticks	air
sees	hoods	who	ricks	fair
bees	woods	what	kicks	lair
could	looks	when	picks	leak
would	books	which	nicks	peak
should	hooks	where	bricks	beak

LESSON XLIII.

girl   floor   ver-y
bird   kill'ed   hap-py
gave   a-bout   moth-er
cage   a-gain   run-ning

See the girl with her bird and cage.
One day her moth-er gave her a bird.
It was run-ning a-bout the floor; and
    a sly cat came and killed it.
The lit-tle girl felt ver-y sad. Then her
    moth-er gave her a new bird.
Now she is hap-py a-gain.

air	leak	licks	eat-ing
fair	peak	ricks	seat-ing
lair	beak	kicks	beat-ing
hair	weak	picks	heat-ing
pair	freak	nicks	heal-ing
stair	speak	wicks	peal-ing
chair	streak	sticks	steal-ing

LESSON XLIV.

air	fly	a-way
bee	ant	a-fraid
paw	from	fly-ing
dish	sil-ly	eat-ing

A pup was eat-ing from a dish. It saw
a bee and an ant.

The bee was not on a bud. It was
fly-ing in the air.

The ant did not fly. An ant can not
fly, but it can run.

The pup put its paw on the ant. But
it ran a-way from the bee.

It was a big bee, and the sil-ly pup
was a-fraid of it.

---

sit-ting	sis-ter	an-gry
fit-ting	blis-ter	hun-gry
hit-ting	mis-ter	seat-ing
sum-mer	sin-ner	beat-ing
hum-mer	din-ner	heat-ing
drum-mer	thin-ner	heal-ing

1st Rd 4

LESSON XLV.

din-ner	a-way
sit-ting	to-day
hun-gry	try-ing
sum-mer	mis-ter

One sum-mer day, a hun-gry fox saw a fat hen, sit-ting on a box lid.

The sly fox said, I can get a din-ner now. But not so.

A big boy saw mis-ter fox, as he was try-ing to get the hen.

The boy ran for his gun. The fox saw the boy go for the gun.

Ah! said mis-ter fox, I can not get a fat din-ner to-day.

If I am not off, the boy may get me. So, a-way ran the fox.

---

stay	wing	that	rives	pound
clay	bring	then	dives	wound
play	string	there	hives	ground

LESSON XLVI.

fast	wing	more
side	string	rise
some	wound	ri-ses
dives	ground	oth-er

See the boy with his new kite. Now it dives in the air.

It will come to the ground. O, it has but one wing!

It will not fly. Put a wing on the oth-er side.

There, that will do. Now let us see if it will rise.

O yes, how fast it ri-ses! Now the string is all wound off.

You may stay and hold it. I will go and get some more string.

---

corn	cow	sack	lass	long
horn	now	back	mass	song
horns	plow	black	grass	strong

LESSON XLVII.

four	cart	lies
draw	hard	works
sleep	quite	drinks
aft-er	white	wa-ter

An ox has two horns. He has four legs and four feet.

The ox can draw the plow. He can draw the cart.

He is quite strong, and works ver-y hard for man.

He has red, or white, or black hair.

He eats grass, and hay, and corn; and he drinks wa-ter.

He lies down on his side to sleep or to rest, aft-er his work is done.

---

sees	light	glow	could	east
flees	night	grow	would	feast
trees	bright	know	should	beast

LESSON XLVIII.

west	trees	al-so
lives	stars	ho-ly
gives	moon	o-bey
made	know	a-live

| takes | keeps | grass | could |
| makes | sleeps | brass | should |

See, the sun is up.

The sun gives us light. It makes the trees and the grass grow.

The sun ri-ses in the east, and it sets in the west.

When the sun ri-ses, it is day; when it sets, it is night.

Do you know who made the sun? God made it.

God al-so made the moon, and all the stars. They give us light by night.

God gives us all we have, and keeps us a-live.

We should love God, and o-bey his ho-ly will.

LESSON XLIX.

sick	what	Wil-ly
each	blind	a-bout
which	mates	Hen-ry
school	James	him-self

free	kept	large	thank
three	slept	barge	Frank

Well, Hen-ry, what do you read a-bout in your new book?

I read of three boys who went to school; James, Frank, and Wil-ly.

Each boy had a fine, large cake.

James ate too much of his cake. It made him sick.

Frank kept his so long, that it was not fit to eat.

But Wil-ly gave some of his to each of his school-mates.

He then ate some him-self, and gave the rest to a poor, old, blind man.

Which, do you think, made the best use of his cake?

LESSON L.

pie	word	sis-ter
nice	on-ly	known
does	speak	sit-ting
says	wants	Ed-ward

Sis-ter Ma-ry, do look at Fi-do. He is sit-ting up, and has a hat on.

Does he not look like a lit-tle boy in the chair? It is on-ly Fi-do.

Shall I ask him to dine with us to-day?

O yes; do ask him to dine with us!

Fi-do, we are to have a ver-y nice pig for din-ner.

Will you take a rib with us? You can have a bit of pie, al-so.

He says not a word. Fi-do can not speak as we do.

Yet he has ways by which he is a-ble to make his wants known.

Ed-ward was the name of the boy.

The name of the dog was Fi-do.

LESSON LI.

goes	a-ny	cru-el
fight	li-on	ti-ger
night	young	call'ed
sheep	strong	al-most

cave	sleep	find	beast	live
caves	sleeps	finds	beasts	lives

The Li-on lives in dark caves. It sleeps there all the day.

At night it goes out to find food. In the day it goes back to its cave.

It can kill an ox, or a sheep, or a ti-ger, or a man.

It can kill al-most a-ny thing it can find.

The Li-on will not eat a-ny thing that it finds dead.

It is not cru-el, but will fight for food, or for its young.

It is so strong, that it can kill al-most a-ny oth-er beast.

It is called the King of Beasts.

LESSON LII.*

latch	li'ed	aft-er	e-ven
catch	tri'ed	sis-ter	sor-ry
hatch	taught	suf-fer	hun-gry
match	caught	broth-er	some-thing

Henry. O Ma-ry! I just saw a large rat in the shed; and old Ne-ro tried to catch it.

Mary. And did he catch it?

Henry. No, sis-ter, Ne-ro did not, but the cat did.

Mary. My cat?

Henry. No; it was the old cat.

---

* Too early attention can not be given to Emphasis. It is during the first year at school that those habits of drawling and monotony in reading are formed, which teachers find so much difficulty in correcting, when the pupil has advanced to the higher classes. This and the following lessons will be found to furnish excellent *drill exercises* in Emphasis

Mary. O, how did she get it? Do tell me: did she run aft-er it?

Henry. No, sis-ter, that was not the way. Puss was hid on the top of a big box, in the shed. The rat stole out; and, pop, she had him.

Mary. Poor rat! It must have been ver-y hun-gry, and came, no doubt, to get some-thing to eat.

Henry. Why, Ma-ry, you are not sor-ry Puss caught the rat, are you?

Mary. No, broth-er, I can not say I am sor-ry she caught the rat; but I do not like to see e-ven a rat suf-fer pain.

ze-ro	al-so	liv-er	o-ver
he-ro	al-ter	riv-er	ro-ver
Ne-ro	al-most	giv-er	clo-ver
a-way	al-ways	ev-er	dro-ver
a-bout	sis-ter	lev-er	oth-er
a-bove	blis-ter	sev-er	moth-er
a-round	mis-ter	nev-er	broth-er

LESSON LIII.

play	hand	sails	old-er
near	sand	made	Wil-ly
with	wood	spade	Ka-ty
what	shore	small	Car-ry

Wil-ly, Ka-ty, and Car-ry are with their mam-ma at the sea-side.

Do you see Wil-ly? Can you tell what he has in his right hand?

O yes, I do see him! Has he not a spade in his hand? It looks like one.

He has a spade in his hand; a small spade, and it is made of wood.

A spade made of wood! Pray, of what use is a spade made of wood?

It is made to play with. There is sand at the sea-side. Wil-ly can dig in the sand, with his lit-tle spade.

Ka-ty has a spade, too. Do you not see it? It lies near her on the sand.

She has laid it down to look at the ship. Can you see the ship? Do you see how fast it sails?

Soon it will be out of sight. Then Wil-ly, Ka-ty, and Car-ry will go home.

Wil-ly is old-er than Ka-ty, and Ka-ty is old-er than Car-ry.

right	found	wade	old-er
light	sound	made	bold-er
sight	hound	blade	cold-er
night	bound	spade	hold-er
bright	ground	shade	mold-er

LESSON LIV.

five	spell	on-ly	Jane
foot	class	nev-er	Co-ra
read	shall	read-er	Ma-ry
hear	three	al-ways	Lu-cy
head	quite	stand-ing	Nel-ly

One, two, three, four, five. Five lit-tle girls, all of the same size; Co-ra, Ma-ry, Nel-ly, Jane, and Lu-cy.

Are they not pret-ty lit-tle girls? How clean and sweet they look.

Lit-tle Co-ra is at the head of her class. See, she is stand-ing up, read-ing to her teach-er.

Shall I tell you why she is at the head?

She al-ways knows her les-son, and nev-er comes late to school.

How old do you think these girls are? They are on-ly six, but they can read quite well in the FIRST READ-ER.

Lu-cy is at the foot of her class now. Last week she was at the head.

One girl can stay at the head a week, if she does not miss.

Was not Lu-cy a good girl to stay at the head a week?

These are all good girls. Will you not try to be good like them?

If you are good, all who know you will love you. God loves good girls.

| clean | these | les-son | teach-er |
| sweet | school | pret-ty | read-ing |

LESSON LV.

look	lead	cri'ed	school
poor	pond	could	ta-ken
dead	there	heard	pa-rent
with	when	Frank	al-ways
kind	loves	Brown	mat-ter

Look, look, is not this Frank Brown?
What can be the mat-ter with him?

The poor boy is dead. He was on his
way to school, when a bad boy met him,
and said:

"Come, Frank, go with me to the pond." "O no," said Frank, "I can not; I must go to school."

But the bad boy told him it was not time to go to school. So Frank went with him to the pond.

Do you see the bad boy? He stands by the side of the man.

Frank fell in-to the pond, and the bad boy could not help him out.

He cried, "Help, help!" A man heard him, and ran to the pond. But when he got there, poor Frank was dead.

What will his pa-rents do when he is ta-ken home dead?

Do not stop to play on your way to school. Do not play with bad boys. They will lead you in-to harm.

their	game	skate	bri-dle
theirs	games	skates	bri-dles
stand	shame	school	pa-rent
stands	shames	schools	pa-rents

LESSON LVI.

long	catch	large	po-ny
name	sleek	house	bri-dle
mane	black	bright	fa-ther
lov'ed	fence	George	be-cause

See this fine po-ny! His name is Jack. Is he not black and sleek?

He can trot, and pace, and run. O, how fast he can run!

Are not his eyes large and bright? Has he not a long mane?

1st Rd. 5.

The name of this lit-tle boy is George. He and his fa-ther live in this house.

Do you see his fa-ther? He stands by the fence.

George is a good boy. When he was ten years old, his fa-ther gave him this po-ny.

George has come out to catch his po-ny. He holds out his right hand to him, and says: "Come, come, Jack!"

But will Jack let George catch him? Will he not run?

O no, he will not run; he will let George catch him. See, he looks at George and does not run.

Did you ev-er ride on a po-ny? It is fine sport.

Do you see the bri-dle George holds in his left hand?

He will put it on his po-ny. Then he can take a ride.

George is kind to Jack, and Jack loves him, be-cause he is kind. The kind and good are al-ways loved.

LESSON LVII.

four	chirp	found	nev-er
bird	leave	where	hap-py
nest	touch	wrong	broth-er
such	break	taught	be-cause

Fanny. O, broth-er, there is such a pret-ty bird! Please get it for me.

Henry. Where, sis-ter? I do not see it. What kind of a bird is it?

Fanny. I do not know what kind of a bird it is, but it will be so pret-ty for my new cage.

Henry. O, I see it now. We have made it leave its nest. Do you not see its nest?

Fanny. O yes, I do. There are eggs in it. We will get the nest, and the eggs too.

Henry. No, sis-ter, we must not touch the bird, nor the nest, nor the eggs.

Fanny. Why, broth-er? I would so much love to have them all.

Henry. But it is wrong to rob a bird of its nest. This bird loves to fly in the air, and make its nest in the trees.

Fanny. Then, broth-er, I do not want the eggs. I did not know it would be wrong to take them.

Henry. It is wrong, sis-ter, to harm the pret-ty birds. We should nev-er think of them but to love them.

God made the lit-tle birds to sing,
　　And flit from tree to tree;
'Tis He who sends them, in the spring,
　　To sing for you and me.

LESSON LVIII.

like	skip	front	snow-y
love	play	light	pret-ty
fond	sees	sheep	com-ing
have	lamb	fleece	be-cause

A sheep and her lamb. What a pret-ty sight!

Do you not love a lit-tle lamb? Would you not like to have one for a pet?

What, a lamb for a pet? Does a lamb make a nice pet?

This lamb is on-ly a few weeks old; but it can run, and skip, and play.

The sheep, or dam, takes good care of it. See how close she lies to it. Does she not seem to love it?

She does love it. She does not like to have it out of her sight.

If she sees a dog com-ing near her lamb, she will run in front of it. Do you know why?

Some dogs kill lit-tle lambs. They will kill sheep too. But sheep can keep the dogs off: the lambs can not.

Would you not feel sad to see a dog kill this lit-tle lamb?

O, what a pret-ty, pret-ty sight,
    To see a lit-tle lamb,
With snow-y fleece, so soft and white,
    At play, be-side its dam.

see	dam	leap	be-side
sees	dams	leaps	be-sides
seem	lamb	take	be-tide
seems	lambs	takes	be-tides

LESSON LIX.

calf	last	could	bos-sy
fast	your	touch	a-fraid
this	hook	guess	a-bout
much	wear	strike	to-ward
think	them	would	teach-er

The last les-son was a-bout a sheep and a lamb. This les-son is a-bout a cow and her calf.

Look at them. Do you think they are as pret-ty as the sheep and lamb?

We call a calf bos-sy. How shy this bos-sy looks!

Do you think it would let you pat it with your hand?

No, it would not. It would run, if you were to try to touch it.

One day it saw a boy com-ing to-ward it. Can you guess what it did?

It ran a-way as fast as it could. The boy ran ver-y fast, too.

The cow saw the boy, and ran to-ward him. She tossed her head, as much as to say: "Do not touch my bos-sy; if you do, I will hook you."

The boy was a-fraid of the cow, and ran off.

Was he not a bad boy, to try to strike a lit-tle calf?

head	strike	look	les-son
what	strikes	looks	les-sons
lamb	hook	learn	read-er
much	hooks	learns	read-ers
touch	thinks	wears	teach-ers

LESSON LX.

must	sight	learn	i-dle
good	front	talks	nev-er
does	laugh	shame	a-gain
wear	dunce	please	teach-er

'O, what a sad, sad sight is this!   A boy with a dunce-cap on his head!

Why does he stand there, in front of the school?   What has he done?

He is a bad boy.   He talks and laughs in school.   He loves to be i-dle, and does not learn his les-son.

Does he not look bad? All the good boys shun him!

Do you think a good boy can love a bad one? Can his teach-er love him?

I think not. No one loves a bad boy. No one can love those who are bad.

This boy tries to hide his face with his hand, for it is red with shame.

Can you see his face? Do you see how he tries to hide it with his hand?

Poor boy! I hope he will be good, and nev-er have to wear a dunce-cap a-gain.

God loves those who are good. If you would please Him, you must al-ways be good and kind.

shun	does	miss	bless
have	done	miss'ed	bless'ed
hope	hide	miss-es	bless-es
front	love	toss	kiss
think	loves	toss'ed	kiss'ed
stand	lov'ed	toss-es	kiss-es

LESSON LXI.

told	fault	soil'ed	spoil'ed
hate	child	pull'ed	sure-ly
word	those	should	broth-er
mean	wrong	clothes	naught-y

Ellen. See, mam-ma, see what puss has done! Bad puss! I shall nev-er like her a-gain.

Mother. Nev-er like puss a-gain? Your pret-ty puss! Sure-ly, you do not mean that. What has puss done?

Ellen. Why, mam-ma, she has spoiled my doll. See, its head is bro-ken, and its clothes are all soiled.

Mother. I am ver-y sor-ry, my dear. But how did puss get your doll?

Ellen. I went to play with broth-er Lew-is, and left doll-y on the floor. Puss saw her there, and pulled her in the dirt. O, how I hate puss!

Mother. Stop, my child, do not use that naught-y word. You should not blame puss, for the fault was all your own.

Ellen. O, mam-ma, how can you say so?

Mother. Be-cause, puss did not know it was wrong to play with your doll. But you knew it was wrong to leave her on the floor.

Ellen. Then, mam-ma, I am sor-ry I struck puss. I shall nev-er do so a-gain, but will love her more than ev-er.

came	wrong	toil′ed	to-ken
name	strong	soil′ed	bro-ken
blame	throng	spoil′ed	spo-ken

LESSON LXII.

flies	shout	joy-ous	trip-ping
swift	games	mer-ry	run-ning
their	skates	in-deed	laugh-ing

Hear the chil-dren gay-ly shout,
"Half past four, and school is out!"
See them, as they quick-ly go,
Trip-ping home-ward o'er the snow.

Mer-ry, play-ful girls and boys,
Think-ing of their games and toys,
Skates, and sleds, and dolls, and books:
O, how hap-py each one looks!

"Now for snow-ball," Har-ry cries,
And to hit his sis-ter tries;
But the ball, so white and round,
Miss-es her, and hits the ground.

Sis-ter Flor-ence, full of fun,
With her lit-tle hands makes one,
And at broth-er Har-ry throws;
Swift it flies, and hits his nose.

"Have I hurt you, broth-er dear?"
Asks his sis-ter, run-ning near;
"Hurt me? no, in-deed," says he,
"This is on-ly sport for me."

Thus these lit-tle chil-dren go,
Trip-ping home-ward o'er the snow
Laugh-ing, play-ing, on their way
Ver-y hap-py, glad, and gay.

cries	gay-ly	miss-es
asks	play-ful	broth-er
sport	quick-ly	Flor-ence
makes	play-ing	think-ing
throws	chil-dren	home-ward

LESSON LXIII.

buy	waste	pit-y	read-y
child	month	man-y	sec-ond
friend	please	read-er	pa-rents
friends	school	teach-er	chil-dren

What! the last les-son? Have we come to the last les-son in the book?

A few months a-go you could not spell. Now, you can read all the les-sons in the First Read-er.

But can you read them well? Can you spell all the words? Did you say yes?

Then you may have the New Sec-ond
Read-er. Are you not glad to be read-y
for a new book?

There are man-y chil-dren whose
pa-rents are too poor to send them to
school. Do you not pit-y them?

They can not have nice books, and learn
to read them, as you do.

Are not your pa-rents kind to send you
to school, and buy new books for you?
Should you not try to please them?

You must not waste your time in school.
Try al-ways to know your les-sons.

If you are good, and try to learn, your
teach-er will love you, and you will please
your pa-rents.

When you go home, you may ask for a
New Sec-ond Read-er.

Take good care of your new book, and
give your old Read-er to some child who
is too poor to buy one.

And now, my lit-tle friends, we must
bid you all a kind Good-by!

THE END.